The vows of]
and
how to keep them

DAVID G. HAMILTON

Artwork by Alistair Jones

SAINT ANDREW PRESS

First published in 1992 by Church of Scotland Education

Published in 2007 by
SAINT ANDREW PRESS
121 George Street, Edinburgh EH2 4YN

ISBN 978 0 7152 0864 9

British Library Cataloguing in Publication Data
A catalogue record for this book is available from the British Library

It is the Publisher's policy to only use papers that are natural and recyclable and that have been manufactured from timber grown in renewable, properly managed forests. All of the manufacturing processes of the papers are expected to conform to the environmental regulations of the country of origin.

Printed and bound by Mackay & Inglis Ltd, Glasgow

Preface

This booklet, for parents and others concerned with Christian upbringing, focuses on the sacrament of baptism.

It is intended as an introduction for parents and is offered in the hope that through word and picture they may be encouraged to think about what is really involved in bringing babies for baptism. The text offers no substitute for a more serious consideration of the most important topic in the Church today. It is no more than a 'mental can-opener', a sort of first aid volume for parents bemused by the apparatus of the church which confronts them whenever the issue of 'The Christening' is raised.

Alistair Jones's cartoons not only lighten the text. They offer their own insights and raise their own questions.

Congratulations!

It's a girl... er... boy... er...

Well, anyway, it's a baby.
What else did you expect?

Here's a suggestion. Give your baby a *name*. It's much better than a number!

Here's another suggestion. Have your baby 'christened' – you know, baptised, church, minister, party, the whole works. But what does this mean?

When a baby is 'christened' it is named as belonging within the Christian family. It all happens in the Sunday service in church when the minister takes the baby in his or her arms and baptises him. Water is sprinkled on the baby's head and the baby is named in the form:

"*Clark Kent*, I baptise you in the name of the Father, the Son and the Holy Spirit".

That's only the beginning. Whether *Clark Kent* will grow up to be a super man – or woman – will depend so much on the parents.

Don't go! It's not as tough as it seems. Read on.

Baptism

When you bring your baby for baptism, he or she will be formally named and in a special ceremony called a *sacrament* received into the Christian Church and shown off to the congregation as the latest recruit to be welcomed into their number.

Baptism is often called the 'Badge of Membership' of the Church.

Parents sometimes find it difficult to grasp that in having their children baptised they are bringing them into the membership of the Church. From that day on, they belong in the Church. They belong to the family of God.

4

Centuries ago, when converts to Christianity were baptised they took on new names in order to emphasise that they were starting a new chapter in life. They wanted to follow Christ and with Christ's help to live a life that would give them meaning and joy. This 'Christian' name was given to mark a new start.

Babies don't need a new start but since the Church baptises not only adult believers but the children of believers what we do in *Infant Baptism* is to emphasise that right from the very beginning the child belongs to Christ. Strictly speaking then, Christian names are the names given at the time of 'Christening' or, as we prefer to call it, baptism.

It ain't necessarily so

You can give your child as many names as you please. Kings and queens do it, why shouldn't you! But take a piece of advice, don't overdo it. Some years ago a fanatical football supporter brought his son for baptism and had him named after the entire Glasgow Rangers first eleven.

Do you believe in magic? If you do, that's too bad because there's nothing magical about baptism. No magic. No tricks.

It's a kind of contract – a deal made between you, the parents, and God. That deal requires you to accept that God cares for you and cares for your baby. And it requires you to promise certain things about how your baby will be brought up. Finally, the 'washing' in water is a sign that a contract has been entered into.

Baptism is a once-and-for-all event. The arrangement, or, to use the jargon, *the covenant*, into which a person enters with God through baptism is for life. If you have been baptised once you need never be baptised again. People may, and frequently do, confirm for themselves in later life the faith into which they were baptised as children. In fact, the whole Church hopes and prays that your child will do just that.

Do remember that the baptism of infants is every bit as meaningful and wholesome as that of adults.

It makes sense then that parents who bring babies for baptism should themselves be baptised. If you have never been baptised, and wish you could be, then it's no big deal. Your minister will happily arrange to baptise you, although he/she may wish to earbash you first. You may even find it interesting!

How did we get into this in the first place?

We baptise people in Church in obedience to the command of Jesus. **Read Matthew chapter 28, verses 16–20.** Baptism is a sign of belonging to Jesus and of being engaged to serve him throughout our lives.

Baptism is the ceremony of entry into membership of the Church. We speak of the **Sacrament of Baptism** because in the action of sprinkling or washing with water we see the sign and symbol of being marked or touched by God's grace. No magic – just an outward sign of the love we hold in our hearts for God and which he holds for us.

For adults who become Christians, baptism is a ceremony of symbolic washing. It represents the washing away of sin and of a past life with values and ways of living that the new convert wishes to renounce. It represents the start of a new life in Christ. It also represents the acceptance of the gift of God's Holy Spirit.

The promise of God to free his people from the grip of sin and to offer them new life in Christ by the giving of his Spirit is extended to believers *and also to their children.* **Read Acts chapter 2, verses 38–9.**

From the earliest times in the history of the Church, Christians have brought their children for baptism.

There was a day when many children died in infancy and parents held the superstitious view that unless the baby was baptised it would not be received into heaven. They sought baptism for their babies as early as possible. There is no foundation for such a view. Baptism is not an insurance policy. God's love is not conditional upon anything we do. We baptise our children because of the command of Jesus and because we witness to the world that with God's help we shall bring them up as Christians.

Once when people brought their children to Jesus his disciples tried to shield Jesus from the hassle of parents and children. Jesus' words on that occasion are very telling. He said, 'Let the children come to me and don't try to hinder them. The Kingdom of God belongs to such as these.'

Read Matthew chapter 19, verses 13–15.

So, to sum up, when we baptise adults or children, we bring them into church membership and place them firmly within the family of God. Baptism has always been the Church's way of helping people set out in the Christian life. All the promises of baptism apply as much to children as to adults and we need look no further than the words of Jesus to see just how much children figure in God's plans.

Wow – what a vow!

Parents bringing their children for baptism will be asked to take vows and make promises just as they did in their marriage service. On this occasion they will be asked to do two things.

The first thing they will be asked to do will be to reaffirm their own Christian faith, the faith into which they were baptised. The question put to the parents will be something like:

> **'Do you believe in one God, Father, Son and Holy Spirit; and do you confess Jesus Christ as your Saviour and Lord?'**

These are the big questions at the heart of the Christian faith. The idea is that those who hold such ideas and beliefs will let them colour and influence the whole of their family life.

But what about those parents who are unsure of what they believe? There are several things you can do:

Take fright and run away ⟨X⟩

OR

⟨X⟩ **Pretend you are saints**

OR

Come clean, admit your confusion ⟨√⟩
(and begin where you are).

Beliefs about God and Jesus take us into very deep issues. If you don't understand the 'idea' of God, then join the club! It's one of the tasks of the Church to help us to discover something of the mystery we call 'God'.

We are not without help!

We have the Bible – and especially the Gospels where we read about Jesus. Jesus, we read, shows us what God is like. In Jesus we see love-in-action. We also see how Jesus, in his life, death and resurrection, draws us closer to God. Read all about it – for yourself – in the Gospels.

Promise?

The second thing required of parents will be their readiness to assume the tasks of being *Christian* parents. So at baptism this second question is posed:

> **'Do you promise, depending on the grace of God, to teach this child the truths and duties of the Christian faith; and by prayer and example to bring *him* up in the life and worship of the Church?'**

Now *there's* an agenda for life! Will you raise your child as a Christian? That means that your child will grow to behave in a Christian way, think in a Christian way and feel in a way that is Christian.

Does that last phrase seem odd? There is a saying that 'Christianity is more caught than taught'. Your child will be expected to 'catch' Christianity from you.

It's a fine theory – but how does it work in practice?

Look again at the promise. The idea is that parents should bring up their children to be Christian through four activities.

These are

Teach what Christians believe

Teach how Christians are expected to behave

Pray for your child and with your child

Be the best possible example(s) of being Christian.

Sure, it's a tall order. There's no way you are going to be successful!

At least, not on your own. That's why the promise says: 'depending on the grace of God'

In all of this you need God's help!

Read Psalm 46, verse 1 and Philippians chapter 4, verse 13.

The people power of the congregation

Congregations at baptisms who think they are there to 'coo' over the baby are in for a surprise.

When the questions presented to the parents are answered by the parents in the form *I/We do*, the minister will then be required to ask the congregation present at the service to make *their* response by showing that they accept their responsibility to support your child and indeed you as parents. Sometimes, the people of the congregation will be asked to stand in their places to show their readiness to support you. In some instances they may be asked to respond to promise questions with the words *We do.* Whatever they do, the members place themselves under oath to play their part in the Christian upbringing of your little one.

This support may be expressed in lots of ways, such as: providing baby creches for parents who wish to attend church services and other church meetings, offering friendship and companionship on an individual basis or in groups, by providing Christian education for children in Sunday Schools and other groups and so on.

No-one is ever a Christian in a vacuum. Christians thrive by sharing their faith and by working together for God.

The vows taken at baptism, as you can see, apply not to the baby's faith but to the faith of the parents and to the congregation as a whole. They are expressions of sincere belief and serious intention on the part of Christian adults.

Under the microscope

Let's place the parents' promise under the magnifying glass. What does it really mean? How will you cope?

How will you teach what Christians believe?

The phrase often used is "teach the truths... of the Christian faith". It means passing on to your child your understanding of Christian ideas and beliefs. It means answering the questions your child will in the years to come ask, such as "How did I get here?", "Who made me?", "What happens when we die?", "Where is heaven?", "How did God make Jesus alive again?", "Who wrote the Bible?", "Why is the Bible so boring?" Chances are that a degree in theology won't help you in this particular task!

There are two principles here that should be followed. *First,* if you don't know the answer to a question, say so! Don't chance your arm. Don't invent your own religion on the spot to get you off the spot. If you don't know the answer, say something like, "That's a good question – let's find out together".

The *second* thing to do is to start *now* finding out more about your faith. There are more books and videos available than you will ever have time to look at. With any luck your newly-baptised child will not ask any awkward questions in the first two years of life so get on with your homework.

There is an old adage that:

You cannot make clear to others
what is not clear to yourself

It applies to parents who teach their children. Think about it.

Teach your child how to behave

Part of the promise made by parents requires them to "teach... the duties of the Christian faith". Every religion has its obligations and its code of behaviour. Christianity is not about rules and regulations and the Bible is certainly not a rule book. At the same time, our Christian faith expects us to show certain qualities of character and behaviour. We are to act with kindness, sensitivity towards others, to avoid malicious gossip, to offer practical help to those in need and to show special concern for the sick, the dying, the lonely and even those who through their own foolishness have brought trouble upon others and upon themselves. It's a tall order, summed up in the words of Jesus, "Love your neighbour as you love yourself".

From the earliest years, help your child to know the importance of love-in-action. "Others before self" is a good working principle.

Prayer

As the years go by, it becomes more and more difficult to find time for the family to be together. If you have not already discovered this, then you soon will. Use the early years of family life to full advantage to make time when you can be together and to make time for God. Prayer is essentially making time for God. Many families find that the children's bedtime is a particularly good time to be together for family chat, stories and to say prayers.

If you are unaccustomed to saying prayers, then don't be put off or feel embarrassed. It is the most natural thing that we should place our lives in God's hands and ask for God's help to live effective and wholesome lives.

There are a few ground rules that might help. Keep the prayers short and the words simple. Cut out all pretentious, 'holy' phrases. Talk with your child about the issues of the day – the joys, the worries, the hopes for tomorrow, and build the simplest of prayers around these ideas. Encourage the little one to take part and be prepared for some surprises.

You are the way

Jesus once said, "I am the true and living way", and people followed him and imitated him and tried to live as he did. Whatever else Jesus is for us, he is an example – a model.

In the same way, you are a model for your child. The way you speak, your mannerisms, your facial expressions, your attitudes and behaviour are a constant source of scrutiny. You are under constant surveillance!

The son of a house burglar turned to theft himself and was set on a life of crime before he left primary school. They all said, "He's a chip off the old block", as though crime was in the genes.

The truth was much more sinister. It wasn't being a chip off the old block so much as living with the old block that was the problem. You are the most important role model(s) your child will ever encounter.

The baptismal promise asks you to bring up your child in the Christian life by your own example.

All the teaching and all the talk in the world will be of little value if it is flatly contradicted by the example you set. The 'do as I say and not as I do' approach simply won't wash.

Begging your pardon, you are not saints. None of us is perfect. But with God's help we can try to be reasonably consistent in the things we say and do. Tempers, gossip, crudeness, selfish acts and such like soon set a pattern for family life. Set yourself worthy standards and keep to them.

In the life of your child *you* are the way.